THIS BOOK RECORDS THE
FIRST YEAR OF

_____

Kitten Record Book

Illustrated by Doreen McGuinness

◆ ◆

Text by Karen Farrington

BLITZ EDITIONS

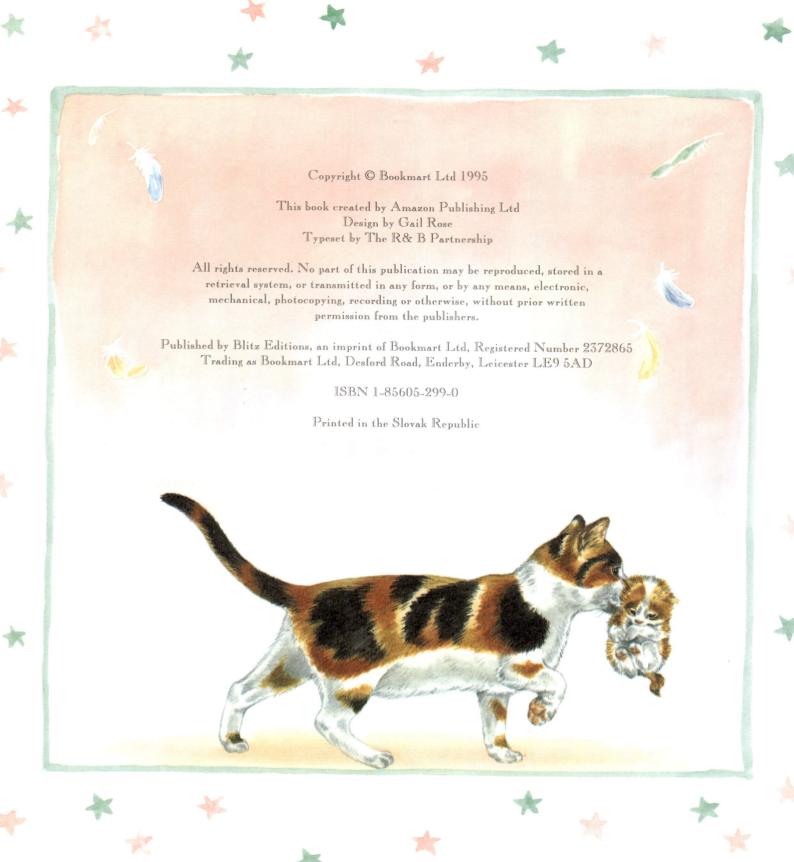

Copyright © Bookmart Ltd 1995

This book created by Amazon Publishing Ltd
Design by Gail Rose
Typeset by The R& B Partnership

All rights reserved. No part of this publication may be reproduced, stored in a retrieval system, or transmitted in any form, or by any means, electronic, mechanical, photocopying, recording or otherwise, without prior written permission from the publishers.

Published by Blitz Editions, an imprint of Bookmart Ltd, Registered Number 2372865
Trading as Bookmart Ltd, Desford Road, Enderby, Leicester LE9 5AD

ISBN 1-85605-299-0

Printed in the Slovak Republic

CONTENTS

✧ ◇ ✧

Pedigree and Family Details 4

Appearance 6

Coming Home 8

Making Friends 10

Playtime 12

Favourite Foods 14

Going Outside 16

Favourite Places 18

Kitten Firsts 20

Grooming 22

Growing Up 24

Being Naughty 26

First Family 28

First Christmas 30

In the Wild 32

Cat Shows 34

Lucky Escapes 36

Feline Friends 38

Mementoes 40

First Birthday 42

Growth Chart 44

Your Cat's Horoscope 46

Pedigree and Family Details

◆ ◆

Your kitten's family tree will be every bit as
fascinating as your own. When you collect your new
pet, be sure to quiz its carer on its family history.
It may not be a blue-blooded aristocat but surely all
cat families have a hint of nobility about them!
Even pet shops can provide some details to take the
mystery out of your new cat's ancestry.
With luck you will be able to build up a picture of
your new addition which you will treasure forever.
Chart the details here.

◆ ◆

Our kitten came from

Frimley, Surrey.

Its birthday was

14 Dec 97

We heard about it when

We chose it because

_he is_

Its mother was

Bedeslea Banoffi

Its father was

Whipplewind Think Pink

The grandparents were

Whipplewind Lilac Minstrel
Antiquity Martini Ripple
Heljac Toby Tobias
Bedeslea Chantilly Lace.

How many were there in the litter?

_3_

What happened to the brothers and sisters?

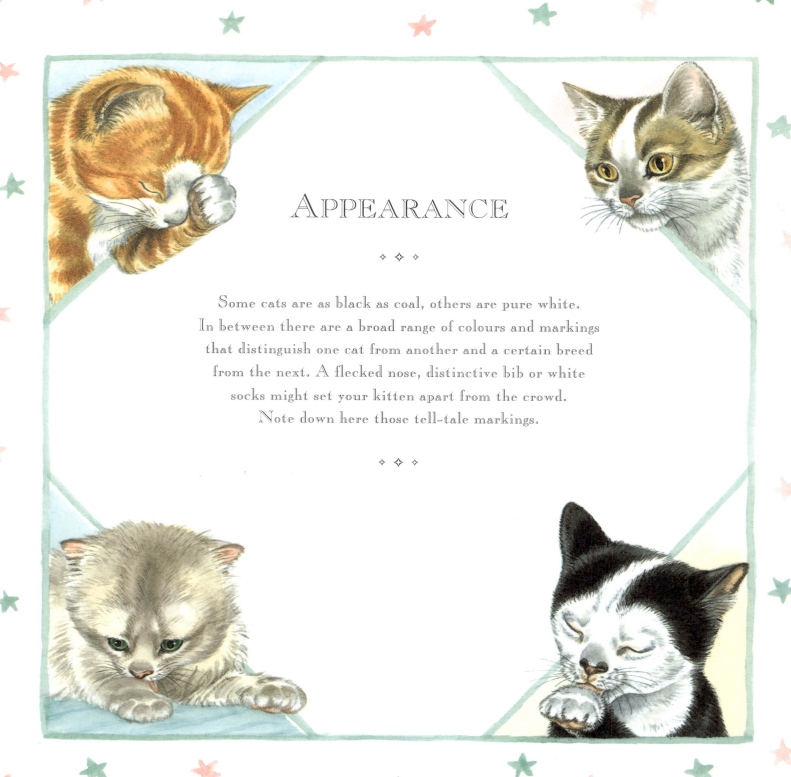

Appearance

◆ ◇ ◆

Some cats are as black as coal, others are pure white.
In between there are a broad range of colours and markings
that distinguish one cat from another and a certain breed
from the next. A flecked nose, distinctive bib or white
socks might set your kitten apart from the crowd.
Note down here those tell-tale markings.

◆ ◇ ◆

Eyes

Face

Ears

Whiskers

Large

Body

Legs

Paws

Tail

Ginger Stripes.

Coming Home

Here's a moment to cherish.
That tiny fluffy bundle arrives home
to share your life for the coming years.
If it is a landmark for you, spare a
thought for the kitten.
This is the most momentous point of its
short life, both thrilling and perhaps a
little alarming. To kitten's eyes, a flat or
house provides an exciting new universe.
As it revels in its new surroundings,
note down how it explores your home.

How kitten travelled home
very well, slept a lot.

Date and time it arrived
14 March 97 at 8-50

What was its very first action?

What did it appear to like best?

Was there anything it was frightened by? Briefly describe its mood
The 2 pet dogs.

Making Friends

◆ ◆

Few people can resist a cute kitten for long. But not all members of the family may be cat lovers at first. Also, there may be other pets in the household to consider. And the existing feline residents of the neighbourhood will need winning over, too. Your puss will learn some important lessons in the art of cat diplomacy. Observe how it copes as it begins to make its way in the world.

How did kitten react to you?

very friendly.

How did it respond to other members of the family?

friendly and loving.

What was the reaction of other pets to the kitten?

barked
hissed & growled. & got excited

And how did it react to the other pets?

hissed & growled.

What was the response of other cats living nearby?

Playtime

✦ ✦ ✦

A cotton reel on string, a bouncy ball, even a shoe lace as it is being tied can provide a romping game for a kitten. For every workaday item there is an adventure to be had for the enterprising young cat who cannot yet tell the difference between toys bought at a pet shop and household objects. If the frantic game of climbing up your dressing gown while you are still in it drives you to distraction, don't worry. Soon the kitten will curl up, exhausted, for a snooze before seeking further sport.

✦ ✦ ✦

List kitten's favourite toys

_____

_____

Describe its antics with household items

_____

What toys did you buy for kitten?

_____

How did it play with them?

_____

_____

Favourite Foods

◆ ◇ ◆

Kittens are ready for food when they are about 32 days old, just over a month. Until then, mother's milk will suffice. Cats are no different to humans when it comes to food. They know what they like and they like what they know. So don't chop and change varieties when they have alighted on one they enjoy. While there are many specially made treats on the market, kittens are also likely to enjoy illicit snacks of cheese, crisps, cake or other luxuries – so be warned before you leave your plate unattended.

Kitten first ate

Go-Cat junior + prawns.

It also enjoyed

For treats we give it

Other foods it likes include

· 15 ·

Going Outside

◆ ◆ ◆

When the time comes to show your kitten the great
outdoors you will be opening the door to an immense playground.
Just as it learned its way around your home, now it must
conquer a brave new world where there are endless adventures
to be had. Trees and bushes to hide in, small garden creatures to
pursue, hosepipes and water sprinklers to play with — keep an eye
on your prowling puss and make a note
of its first steps into the unknown.

◆ ◆ ◆

When did your kitten first go outside?

_____

What was its first reaction when you opened the door?

_____

_____

_____

What were its first actions outside?

_____

_____

_____

What obstacles did it meet?

_____

How did it overcome them?

_____

Favourite Places

⋄ ⋆ ⋄

Soon your kitten will have established its haunts outside. It doesn't take long for a feisty feline, no matter now small, to sort out the best vantage points in the neighbourhood from which it can keep a sharp eye on things. In the house, too, there are warm spots like the airing cupboard, the radiator shelf or in front of the fire which are like magnets to cats. Then you will find it hard to dislodge your comfortable kitten from its favourite cosy nest.

⋄ ⋆ ⋄

Outside, kitten's favourite places were

———————————————————————

———————————————————————

Inside, kitten's favourite places were

———————————————————————

———————————————————————

Kitten Firsts

◆ ◇ ◆

There are plenty of 'firsts' for your kitten to notch up on its journey to adulthood. Some of them will change its life, some will improve yours. As each milestone is achieved, look back and see how far your little kitten has come in life.

◆ ◇ ◆

When did kitten begin to use the cat litter tray?

———————————————

When did kitten master the cat flap?

———————————————

When did kitten sleep in
its own bed?

___

How did kitten react when you first
gave it a collar?

___

When did kitten start to stalk
other animals?

___

How did kitten first react to rain

___

to sunshine

___

to snow

___

Grooming

✦ ✧ ✦

While loving cat-owners might indulge in brushing and combing their pet's fur, a cat or kitten is capable of looking after its own coat. Felines like to preen their fur not only to make it clean but also to flatten ruffles for warmth. In hot weather, they lick saliva onto their toasting coat so, when it evaporates, they are cooled. Grooming by a loving carer comes into its own, however, with long haired cats or during the moulting season, to prevent cats getting hairballs in their stomachs.

✦ ✧ ✦

How does your cat groom itself (watch closely to see if there is a preferred order of priority)?

_____

_____

_____

_____

How does it enjoy your grooming with a brush or comb?

_____

How does it react to a bath?

_____

Growing Up

◆ ◇ ◆

At six months old, kittens are already fully grown and well-able to fend for themselves. In the company of humans, however, they will remain kitten-like until well into adulthood, viewing their owner as 'mum'. Look back through this book and compare your cat at six months to the tiny kitten you first knew. Then note down here details at six months and again at a year – to make a record of how your kitten develops.

◆ ◇ ◆

AT SIX MONTHS:-

Describe its coat

_____

Describe its food

_____

How is its general behaviour?

_____

How has it changed since
you first brought it home?

_____

AT ONE YEAR:-

Describe its coat

_____

Describe its food

_____

How is its general behaviour?

_____

How has it changed since it
was six months old?

_____

Being Naughty

◆ ✦ ◆

Given the chance, kittens are
mischievous minxes. Turn your back for
a minute at the breakfast table and they
will slurp your cereal. Leave them for
too long in one room and you could
come back to find your
ornaments rearranged on the floor
by your cavorting kitten.
There are thousands of ways for a kitten
to get up to no good. How and where did
your tiny tiger transgress?

Date and place

What kitten did

Date and place

What kitten did

Date and place

What kitten did

First Family

◆ ◆ ◆

In the blink of an eye, kittenhood has gone and that scrap of fur that you proudly brought home has become a young adult ready to have a family of its own. The thought of a collection of adorable kittens around the house is often hard to resist — even if it occurs by accident. However, it becomes increasingly difficult to find loving homes for hosts of kittens. Sooner or later, many cat owners find themselves consulting a vet about neutering.

◆ ◆ ◆

How old was your pet when it fathered or gave birth to kittens?

How many kittens were in the litter?

Where and when were they born?

What colours were they?

When did they open their eyes (usually after a week)?

Which was your favourite?

Did you keep any?

First Christmas

◆ ◆ ◆

Just as the eyes of a child sparkle with glee when the tinsel and lights go up on the tree, so a kitten will also be tantalised with the seasonal trimmings. Batting a decoration, climbing a pine branch or even nibbling on a foil-wrapped chocolate is as joyous to a kitten as the prospect of Santa is to a human infant. Describe in full how your young cat enjoyed its first Christmas.

◆ ◆ ◆

With which decorations did kitten play?

_____

_____

What gifts did it receive?

_____

_____

What did it have for dinner?

_____

_____

Special memories of that day

_____

_____

In the Wild

◆ ✧ ◆

In your eyes, a kitten may seem a model pet, all tame and tender. But don't forget that it has a history dating back some 9,000 years, much of it spent in the wild. You can still see in its behaviour examples of this glorious heritage. When did your kitten:

First trample its feet in your lap?
(A movement it would have used to stimulate milk from its mother)

_____

_____

◆ ✧ ◆

First rub around your legs?
(To scent-mark.)

_____

_____

First claw at the furniture?
(To remove old claw casings and to scent-mark.)

_____

_____

First chatter its teeth when hunting?
(Practising its killing bite, not witnessed in all cats.)

_____

_____

First jump on its hind legs to greet you?
(To attempt a ritual face-to-face greeting,
common among cats)

_____

Cat Shows

◆ ◇ ◆

Owners of pedigree cats are frequently delighted to show off their fine felines at a show. However, cat shows are not just the preserve of the pampered pedigree pet. Many shows have sections especially for moggies while village fetes also cater for well-loved kittens and cats. If you get the chance to show off your kitten or cat, make a note of the details here.

◆ ◇ ◆

Venue	Venue	Venue
Date	Date	Date
Type of show	Type of show	Type of show
Placing	Placing	Placing
Prize	Prize	Prize

Lucky Escapes

◆ ✦ ◆

It is said a cat has nine lives. And often kittens need every one
of them to survive! Curious cats are forever getting into scrapes,
being trapped in tall trees and in the path of wind-blown doors.
Note down the hair-raising moments your cat has known.

◆ ✦ ◆

Date and place

_____

_____

Lucky escape

_____

_____

Date and place

_____

_____

Lucky escape

_____

_____

Feline Friends

◆◇◆

Padding, prowling (and occasionally howling) cats are a familiar sight in most neighbourhoods. When your kitten goes out and about, it will encounter a host of new felines, both friend and foe. Perhaps it will then bring one of them home to meet you. List those cats who feature in the everyday life of your cat.

◆◇◆

Friends

Foes

Mementoes

◆ ◆ ◆

Size-wise your kitten is making strides.
So why not gently press one or more of
its muddy paws onto a piece of paper,
allow to dry and then stick it in here.
It will be a memento to treasure for ever.
You could also gather some fur from its
bed and stick it behind clear, adhesive
tape as another reminder of kitten's
younger days.

◆ ◆ ◆

◆ Kitten's paw print ◆

◆ Kitten's fur ◆

First Birthday

✦ ✦ ✦

It might be difficult to pinpoint the exact date your kitten was born. But the day you brought it home to stay will be etched in your mind for ever. Why not celebrate it on the first anniversary and every year after that with a special treat? Then your cat will really feel one of the family!

✦ ✦ ✦

Date of anniversary

_____

How we celebrated

_____

Gifts we gave to our kitten

_____

_____

_____

Growth Chart

◆ ◇ ◆

At first your kitten is a furry, purry ball which sits pert and alert in the palm of your hand. Before you know it kitty will have grown to be a bold cat-about-town, with plans to make, tricks to play and friends to meet. The physical development of your kitten tells its own amazing tale. Note down how it grows below, to provide a lasting memento of this magical time.

◆ ◇ ◆

Date	Date	Date
Length of cat, nose to tail	Length of cat, nose to tail	Length of cat, nose to tail
Length of tail	Length of tail	Length of tail
Weight	Weight	Weight

Your Cat's Horoscope

◆ ◇ ◆

Who said horoscopes were for humans only?
Take your cat's birthday and see whether or not
it is true to its star sign.

◆ ◇ ◆

◆ Capricorn ◆
Ambitious, persevering, restrained, aloof, enjoys routine.

◆ Aquarius ◆
Independent, relaxed, rebellious, loyal, seeks challenges.

◆ Pisces ◆
Imaginative, stoic, home-loving, gullible, passes the time with creative play.

◆ Aries ◆
Bold, brash, energetic, physically strong, thrives with stimulation.

◆ Taurus ◆
Calm, cautious, placid, persistent, passionately affectionate.

◆ Gemini ◆
Bubbly, quick-witted, manipulative, prone to boredom.

◆ Cancer ◆
Moody, emotional, motherly, sensitive, needs security.

◆ Leo ◆
Friendly, brave, buoyant, good humoured, a lover of the lazy life.

◆ Virgo ◆
Gentle, orderly, precise, fussy, enjoys a cuddle.

◆ Libra ◆
Diplomatic, calm, co-operative, indecisive, naturally sociable.

◆ Scorpio ◆
Secretive, understanding, intuitive, popular yet one of life's loners.

◆ Sagittarius ◆
Mischievous, boisterous, adventurous, impatient, the cat's clown.